In This Burning World

ALSO BY MARY MACKEY

Poetry

The Jaguars That Prowl Our Dreams: New and Selected Poems 1974–2018
Marsh Hawk Press, *Winner of the 2019 Eric Hoffer Award for Best Book Published by A Small Press*
Travelers With No Ticket Home, Marsh Hawk Press
Sugar Zone, Marsh Hawk Press, *Winner of the PEN Oakland Josephine Miles Award for Literary Excellence*
Breaking the Fever, Marsh Hawk Press
The Dear Dance of Eros, Fjord Press
Skin Deep, Gallimaufry Press
One Night Stand, Effie's Press
Split Ends, Ariel Press

Nonfiction

Creativity: Where Poems Begin, Marsh Hawk Press

Novels

The Village of Bones, Lowenstein Associates
The Widow's War, Berkley Books
The Notorious Mrs. Winston, Berkley Books
The Year the Horses Came, Harper San Francisco
The Horses at the Gate, Harper San Francisco
The Fires of Spring, Penguin
Season of Shadows, Bantam
The Kindness of Strangers, Simon & Schuster
A Grand Passion, Simon & Schuster
The Last Warrior Queen, Putnam
McCarthy's List, Doubleday
Immersion, Shameless Hussy Press

Novels Published under the name "Kate Clemens"

Sweet Revenge, Kensington Books
The Stand In, Kensington Books

In This Burning World

Poems of Love and Apocalypse

Mary Mackey

Marsh Hawk Press
East Rockaway, New York·2025

Marsh Hawk books are published by Marsh Hawk Press, Inc., a not-for-profit corporation under section 501(c)3 United States Internal Revenue Code.

Book Design: Susan Quasha
FIRST EDITION

LCCN: 2024058394

ISBN 9798987617762

on the far shore of grief lies hope
just keep swimming

M.M.

CONTENTS

PREFACE

Poems of Love and Apocalypse

Welcome to the New Planet. The Old Planet, the familiar one we human beings have inhabited for nearly 12,000 years since the end of the last Ice Age, is disappearing. The glaciers are melting, the forests burning, the seas and rivers rising, the great winds blowing. What will the future be like? How will those of us who are young live in this new world taking shape under our feet? How will those of us who are old describe what has been lost, so generations to come—who have never seen an unbleached coral reef or a glacier—can understand the Earth we left behind?

There are no easy answers to these questions, but that shouldn't stop us from trying to imagine what life will be like on the New Planet. And so I offer you these poems, which are about two kinds of burning: the burning of apocalypse and the burning of love. The apocalyptic burning is obvious. Look at any newsfeed, read any scientific study, and it stares you in the face. The burning of love is more nuanced. If we can't undo the effects of climate change, we still can choose to love and care for another with passionate kindness and passionate devotion. We can burn with the determination to shelter and comfort those who have lost everything. We can choose to reach out to one another; create places where grief cannot enter; love one another as we love ourselves.

Mary Mackey

PART I
In This Burning World

Pillar of Smoke/Pillar of Fire

such a short path

I thought it would be longer
I thought I would be dead
before we reached the end

but here we are
in the Promised Land of broken promises
limping across a bridge of ivory
made from the spines
of all the animals
who have ever gone extinct

the green hills lie behind us
the drowned cities
that once were our joy
quiver beneath saltwater and despair
ice is not even memory
and the forests
sleep in charred tangles
like petrified jackstraws

in front of us lies a desert
that goes on forever
its wind dries our breath
its dust fills our mouths
its sand burns our feet like hot charcoal
there is no peace here
no water
no manna
no golden calves
no books made of honey
to sweeten our tongues
no commandments carved in stone

no gods waiting to save us
from ourselves

Ashes

there was another planet once
a garden   an orchard   a joy
a cool   green refuge
filled with golden light
that lay on our lips like honey

the sun has turned to blood
our eyes sting   our throats are raw
there are ashes in our hair
ashes on our hands
ashes on our tongues
the bitter taste of ashes in our mouths

we hope if we die by fire
we will wake in a world
where all this will be reversed
but when we stare into the river
the light that flows between
the trunks of the cottonwoods
eats at the current
like a bank of white-hot flames

Burnt Offering

the sun is scorching the horizon
each step we take
crackles like candy wrappers
above us the stars float
grimy and abandoned as cinders

in this city of our abandoned bodies
death leads the way
pipping on a flute of bone

Leaving the City

we moved
like swimmers
who had given up
and slipped sideways
out of time

we needed to look at the stars
but tall buildings
had shattered the sky

driven forward by a bitter
taste on our tongues
that left our stomachs empty
one   by   one
we stumbled down
to the edge of the ocean
where great waves
were slowly eating away
the land

When Mirrors Are Reversed

When mirrors are reversed
we will walk together through skeleton forests
along rivers that boil like molten glass

behind us   ghost panthers
will stalk us through the dust of our cities
gathering up our unborn children
and unraveling our dreams

the skies will be filled with fish
and the oceans will be filled with crows
our mouths will be filled with dust
and we will not drown
we will smother

The Crystal Falcon

"July 2024 was the hottest month ever recorded on Earth."
National Oceanic and Atmospheric Administration

heat shadows fall on the sidewalk
burning our footprints into the cement
like those gray silhouettes
left on the walls at Hiroshima
  a child chasing a ball
  a dog pulling on a leash
  two lovers spinning to face one another
  as a second sun rises over the city
  and the world goes white

on the trees   the ghost leaves
dangle like mute wind chimes
and the earth stretches
still and hot for as far
as we can breathe

over our heads
the empty sky
hovers like a crystal falcon

tell me, lovc
what sun-scarred thing
will walk out of the glitter
that is playing across
the western horizon tonight
like liquid steel

Memories of Snow

"Snow cover across the nation is only at 5 percent—
the lowest since records began."
The Washington Post, December 3, 2021

quiet as breath
cold on our lips
as promised kisses
the sun shaped it
into mounds of diamonds
spires of ice
ephemeral cathedrals

today the paths we wander down
burn beneath our feet
the rivers are dry
the grass is gasping
in the distance
the mountain peaks
shimmer like steel

tonight as we sleep in each other's arms
dust will blow over us
like a windborne penance

Fire Next Time

Earth's a convection oven
New Delhi's a gas chamber
birds are falling out of the sky
California's burning
and we're up to our ankles in green foam

the wet bulb temperature of Houston
is steaming wildcat oilwell drillers
like organic kale
and just outside of Phoenix
355,000 recreational vehicles
are baking climate refugees like cookies

the coral reefs are whiter than your back teeth
the bones of the great cats
lie in the jungle
like discarded marimbas
even the damned cockroaches are turning belly up

The Long Light

the long light
lies on the grass like yellow
dust

the old oaks   monstrous
and twisted   shed deadly
splinters

a flock of birds
silently passes over us

Huracán

we found your legs
under your skirt
one made of wind
the other a serpent

we should have worshipped you
but we were proud and foolish
used you badly
never loved you

now you have found us
wound around us
smothered us between
your breasts

each summer you will come back
scrape the earth clean
toss our cities into the sea

Hurricane/Huracán

you made us from clay
and we melted
you made us from wood
and we burned
you made us from flesh
and we destroyed ourselves

The Goddess With One Leg

you whirled for 36 hours
in one place
and then came to us
saying: *you will lie under water*
under rubble   under me

I speak in many tongues
I will suck the air from your lungs
I would dance on your graves
but you will have none

O Pantanal Em Chamas/The Pantanal in Flames

"In the Pantanal, the world's largest tropical wetland,
3,372 fires were registered from January to June 2024,
a 2,000% bump from last year's 150 fires."
Mongabay Series: Amazon Conservation

ao meo-dia
at high noon

the apple snails
and marsh deer
giant river otters
hyacinth macaws
crowned eagles
maned wolves
bush dogs
caimans
tapirs   egrets
ibis   anteaters
golden plovers
ocelots and
green anacondas

será dado
will be given
como um holocausto
as a burnt offering

air will turn to milk
and breath will turn to butter

no prophet will stumble
down from the Andes
to save them

and no one will pluck
manna off the
burning cat's claw thorns

the great trees
will wail and sway
in a wind of flames
that will lick their trunks
like demonic jaguars
and a golden calf
will dance around
the people

The New Planet

the wind has turned waspish
our shadows have shrunk
to the size of spiders
the sun burns under
our tongues like a hot ember
and the cities we
left behind
have fallen into the sea
spraying shards of glass
like droplets from a hose

today a new beauty
is being born
and in it
there will be no room
for us

Dark Angels

the clouds massed
above us like lost ships
and the sky was a
vast blue cathedral
laced with the scaffolding
of our brains

mysterious birds
flew across our corneas
and the light was long and low
threaded with the shadows
of tall finger-limbed oaks
that bent over us
like dark angels

generation after generation
lovers lay in each other's arms
filled with a joy that made them dizzy
whispering *this is forever* *this will never pass*
and mothers brought forth
children into a present
that was slowly drifting
away from them
like a small wooden boat

how will we ever
stop mourning
ever understand
this new planet
map it
love it
make it our own

The Emperor Contemplates His Solitude on an ice floe in Antarctica

an emperor penguin
stands staring across
a vast white emptiness
mottled with golden light

as the Emperor contemplates his solitude
his world is melting
and the lands his ancestors traversed
on their long ancient migrations
are disappearing into a gray ocean
of pearl-colored waves and opalescent fog

what does an Emperor think when he feels
his world disappearing beneath his feet?

does he struggle to imagine the cause
or does he simply stand at the edge
of this great catastrophe
with a mind as empty and serene
as a sheet of ice

PART II

Mocking Cassandra

Mocking Cassandra

they mocked her when she said
cities would go under
rocks melt   oceans boil
birds fall from the sky
beaches be ankle-deep in green foam

they laughed at her for laying in stores
filling cans with water
called her crazy   cracked
drove her from town to town like Mirabai
in rags with a begging bowl

when she kept crying   look! it's getting closer!
wet bulb 35C!   brownouts!   blackouts!
famine!   war!   pestilence!
people cooked in their beds!
they shook their heads   rolled their eyes
put AirPods in their ears   watched the playoffs
bought virtual genitals and hooked up in the Metaverse
ate potato chips and smoked weed
shot up high schools
and made videos of their cats playing the piano

poor, crazy Cassandra, they said
hypervigilant, hysterical, neurotic
just shut her up   she's spoiling the party

but she could see darkness
running around the rim of the horizon
see the light blurring
see the end of dishes washed by machines
air conditioning   ice cubes
the easy way you could call people
on the other side of the planet

hear their voices   see their faces
tell them you loved them

I Am the Prophet Who Stands on the Tracks

At the age of sixty
I was given the gift of prophecy
before that I lived blindly
stumbling toward the future
with outstretched hands
suddenly I began to see everything in fine detail
the curl of burning linoleum
the shudder of melting windows
the panicked fire ants
scurrying away from the heat
with their eggs held over their heads

the sun rose   set   and rose again
in a fiery cloud shaped like a tulip
and the stock market became a serpent
that curled back on itself

I saw all of us standing together on iron rails
holding each other's hands
as a black train hurtled towards us

the rain was made of glass
and the air was liquid fire
my phone floated in front of me
just out of reach
and constantly it chanted
missile incoming
missile incoming
this is not a drill
repeat this is not a drill

Jump! I cried
but no one listened

I am your fool
your madwoman
your cut-rate Cassandra
who speaks a truth
no one believes

I am the prophet who stands on the tracks
listening to her phone
holding your hands
and watching the headlight
of the oncoming train
grow larger

Crown of Thorns

In the park her lover designed
the Cassandra of the tropics
wanders among the jacarandas
while overhead flocks of clouds
shaped like white-furred parrots
skim south along the edge of Guanabara Bay

the future, she cries, *is coming like a great wind*
Rio will drown
and Christ will float above the waters
his stone arms outstretched
over the last spires
of the last churches
which the saints will call
a new crown of thorns

how beautiful the final moments of
this great city will be
as the blue wash of the waves
streams over its underwater jungles
and dead men on rented bikes
ride below its sun-fired surface
past children with faces pale as the conch shells
the mães-de-santos cast for divination

You who are setting the world on fire
Wake up

turn toward Corcovado
and beg the Earth our Mother
to save us   before we all sink
beneath our lost   abandoned   drowning
Christ

Prophecy of the Trees

we are a single living body
a sacred beast without a name
ten billion white candles
topped with green flame
sucking water from the earth
speaking a language you don't understand
wide as infinity
silent as the moment that comes
just after death

we toss your planes into the clouds
fill your nights with a million moving shadows
create our own weather

roots tangled
vines twisting around our trunks
like a snake of stars
we are as unstoppable as rain

Listen   Here is our prophecy:

when the songs of the birds
become ghost songs
and the frogs go mute
and the cicadas stop humming
when nothing walks   or talks
or wanders among us but you
and the only sound in the jungle
is the sound of your voices
we will become the great love you lost
the hope you abandoned
the fires that burn you
the ashes that fill your lungs

Cytherea

Quivering fins
ridged like rakes
a sliding, gill-chambered tongue
the inside of her mouth
is yellow and blue
barracuda silver
sweet as red mullet
stripped with black and green
with peacock flounder teeth
pink and sharp and quick

Cytherea is angry
that we have poisoned her oceans
at night she climbs the waves
straddles the white foam
and calls to her whales
"are you cat food yet?"
she howls
"have they made you
into lipstick and soup?"

She is unforgiving
and methodical
when a dolphin gets tangled
in a tuna net
she grieves
when a single cell of green algae dies
she knows it

She has picked the brains
of all the philosophers who ever drowned
looking for the causes of human folly
she has mastered the concept of original sin
and thinks there may be something to it

she is acquainted with the theory of eternal forms
which holds that if the oceans of earth die
the idea of oceans will persist unchanged
in some godly sphere of boredom and perfection
but the only oceans Cytherea cares about
are these
bitter and dirty
salty and dying
these small mortal oceans
it makes her weep to see them

the rusting barrels of nuclear waste
drive Cytherea to distraction
she plots revenge
with the cunning of a shark—she
who was so peaceful
that the Phoenician sailors
wrote odes to her patience
calling her dove soft
smoother than their wives
purple skinned and lovely
as the harbor of Tyre
when the shellfish blossom
oh lovely sea goddess
they wrote,
we move across your belly
like bridegrooms
singing your praises

Now she sits in a dark cave
consorting with morays
sipping poison drinks
concocted from the venom
of Australian stone fish
counting the tankers
that rumble overhead

breathing the oil-fouled water
assimilating the toxins
through her seaweed soft skin
she is not pleased
she is not amused

Cytherea is planning something
down there
something she tells only
to the spiny batfish
and sea dragons
perhaps she has decided
to call back the oxygen
and leave us gasping
perhaps she has decided
to melt her ice caps
rise and take back all the cities
that ever emptied sewage
down her throat
perhaps she has decided to show us
a mercy we don't deserve—
but don't count on it

Cytherea
the flowers we throw to you
come back oil-soaked
and dying
we stand on your beaches
calling you up
but you no longer appear
at our feet you scatter
pieces of styrofoam cups
tin cans, beer bottles, hunks of insulation,
stinking fish and dead birds
and sometimes a jellyfish
pulsing and dying

like a punctured soap bubble
like a human heart
gone bad

The Goddess of Burning Hair

I am your fire dancer
your goddess of burning hair
your monkey gatherer
bird rescuer
rider of the Great River
weaver of lianas
drinker of viper venom
keeper of the rainforests
and of the margins of the rainforests
and of the great drowned forests
that sleep beneath the flaming trees

I can call down the stars
that slither across your skies
move the five panthers that hold up the earth
summon the six jaguars that eat the moon

I can show you visions
of your own destruction
as easily as I can draw breath

come closer
hear my prophecy:

She who you trample
will trample you
She who you burn
will burn you
She who you poison
will rise resurrected
and outlast you

the ice will return
the pure air will return

but you will not return

I warn you: stop it   stop it now

full stop

PART III

Vampire Time

Here/Not Here

"On March 11, 2020, The World Health Organization declared COVID-19 a Pandemic." CDC Museum COVID Timeline

cafés full
45-minute waits
hot soup   grilled shrimp
children running between the tables

now   empty

West Village
the deli the library
people swarming out of
the 14th street subway station

empty

cars rusting
a sheet of white paper
flapping like the wing of a wounded bird
water in the subway tunnels
blind fish white as bones
swimming in circles

at the solstice
a Stonehenge of tall buildings
blinding light
heat unbearable

cactus in Washington Square Park
dust clouds marching toward
Ellis Island

at night   a city so bright

you can see it from space
lost in a darkness so thick
it sticks in your lungs
like the breath of ghosts

Back In 2020

how can you understand what it was like

how we were all together
and all alone
how each of us had books with our lives
crossed out   our plans cancelled
our imagined futures
unimagined

how sometimes we
felt we were in dark tunnels
with trains coming toward us
from all directions
how the bodies of our friends
were kept in trucks
and parks were ploughed
with souls

the terror is easy
to describe   the long restless
nights   the sudden awakenings
the way we reached out in
darkness and pulled back
empty hands
the way we clung to one another
every morning like people
on an ice floe being
swept out to sea

but how do we describe the joys
the way spring came back
and the bees kept plunging
drunkenly into the sage
coyotes roamed our cities
mountain lions slept on our roads

and we walked under skies
bluer than they had been
in sixty years   breathing air
so fresh it went to our heads
like wine

how can you understand our guilty
pleasures   people sitting on their front
porches again   small children and their
parents walking together every afternoon
hand in hand

night after night
day after day
a great   silent   peace
fell over us
like a blanket of roses
and we felt a gentleness
that made it seem as if
we were living
in a world   where words
had never been
invented

you know now where we
were going
and how all this turned
out   but we didn't know
there was no end we
could see   no other life
we could imagine
only this one   here
now
this life we grasped with clean
hands   breath after
labored breath

Bats

they come at twilight
on wings so thin-veined
and whorled   that moonlight
shines through them
like cold fire

fluttering   gliding
slapping the wet air
clicking   howling
singing like drunken songbirds
in warbling   high-pitched voices
hunting every small thing
that flees and hides

imagine for a moment
god is a bat
or that bats have created a god
in their own image

what paradise would they have been expelled from
what are they trying to tell us
as they cross and re-cross the night

Vampire Time

that moment between fire and darkness
darkness and dust
when the limbs of the oaks loom like guillotines
over houses heated beyond bearing
and the leaves breathe in long rustling gasps
and the wind blows pale grains of sand
along the gutters in a mockery of rain

that moment when the sun
singes the horizon
in a conflagration
that sends flocks of crows
careening across purpling infinity
like shards of coal
and the blood drums in your throat
begging for release
begging for just one more evening
on the old familiar planet
with its soft days
and cool nights

vampire time
that hour when the strange becomes familiar
and the familiar becomes strange
when the living are burned
and the dead   resurrected
come streaming across the asphalt
like pale fire   so thin and transparent
you feel as if you could step through them
into another world

All Day the Great Ships Move East

all day the great ships move east
balanced on a blue horizon
like dancers   as they
thread their way out to sea
between jungle-green hills that
dip like bowing saints
into an ocean so clear
you can see your toes

at last at sunset they carry their cargos
into a golden sweep of gilded
whitecaps and blood-red waves
lighting up like candelabras that dance
across the drawing darkness
as if to dispel all doubt that somewhere
there exists a merciful creator
who painted the world into being
with a brush made from the hair of angels

at dawn a new fleet appears
sliding into the port over the backs
of whales like a necklace of dark
hallucinations that quiver
and shift in the rising
heat as their wakes
spread out behind them like
shrouds and the water
turns blue
beneath their keels

in their hulls they carry
a white powder that causes
death   insanity   and a grief
beyond bearing

come   my love
let us go down to the beach
and watch the ships

Pale Riders

again the pale riders
will come out of the East
dragging the mountains
behind them
and the leaves will rustle
with the songs of the dead
carried on warm winds

we will be left
with the sound of a
single guitar lilting
the sound of panthers
walking on soft pads

the sound of lost things
looking for themselves

The Temple of Bel

they come from the ruins

some with the heads of foxes
some with the heads of saints
some shrunk to the size of a pebble
some larger than the sea

walking on water
walking right side up and
upside down
eyes shining like steel
hands bright as blades

some with roots
some with nothing
some who can write with
their tongues

blue lipped
choked with salt and indifference
drowning in a love so distant
it might as well be
hate

The Long Warm Tongue of Your Future

if you could sense your future
prowling behind you
feel its hot breath on your shoulders
smell its rank scent   hear its low cough
you wouldn't ask what's coming next

do you hear that sound like locked breaks
coming from the jungle

your future has thirty teeth
its tongue is long and warm
and it hunts by night

How To Write Novels

kiss snakes
channel Cassandra
go into a trance and talk to Willa Cather
Sheena Queen of the Jungle
and all the bad boys you ever let into your bed

swallow cyanide-laced peach pits
and run against the wind
while chanting
the major provisions
of the revised 1945 tax code

drink ink   eat library paste
look into the future
using three dogs
a dead carp
and a pair of broken ducks

never use novel-writing software

who the hell needs it?

the whole world crashed
years ago

PART IV

The Beauty of the Old Planet

Remembering the Old Planet

fields of ripe wheat
stalks bowing in unison

the shining scales of a cutthroat trout
the scent of wild fennel
the smell of rain and dust

the vibrating wings
a dragonfly
as it conjures up
rainbows with every stroke

a flight of blue macaws
a troop of golden-maned monkeys
a single live oak
leafed with black crows
against a blood-red sky

let's embrace all this
while we can

remember it

try to describe it to our
children

The Beauty of the Old Planet

let's cherish the beauty of the Old Planet
its tall glass towers
and underground cities
long white beaches
and soft forest floors

the way its sky arches over us
free of smoke
so clear and deep
it looks like the sides
of a bottomless blue cup

let's walk together one last time
through its unburned forests
toward wild rivers that run
to the sea
remembering cold spring days
cool summer mornings
snow that melts in our hands
ice that etches crystal leaves
on our windowpanes

sidewalks we can walk on
without burning our feet

Jerusalem Revisited

today
just for a moment
I forgot which wars
we were fighting
who had been shot
who had been slaughtered
who was President
and how much of the arctic ice
cap had melted

on a branch above me
I saw a sparrow
who knew no history but her own
and for the space of two breaths
maybe less
I lay down my bow of burning gold
and broke my arrows of desire

Close Up

red gold
amaranth amber
umber magenta
sapphire violet
viridian malachite
and fifty more colors
only the bees can see

oblate pointed
thirty-four veins running
toward stem and branch
and trunk
sucking water
a hundred feet up into the air
from a hidden river
so black even the fish
are blind

only a single leaf
easy to overlook
smaller than a scrap of paper
a whirl of dust
an open hand

I Knew People Born 130 Years Ago

they taught me to feel the earth
breathe beneath my feet
trace the furrows of a white oak
with my fingers
slide my palms
along the smooth trunk of a beech tree
crush a single wild strawberry
under my tongue
walk west
under a summer sunset
that streaked the sky
like frozen lightning

The Jungle Is a Gentle Beast in My Bed

the jungle is a gentle beast in my bed
fur soft as quetzal feathers
eyes like opals
twisting its vines around my body
with whispered caresses

when I am faithful and constant
it lives inside me
naked and pure
as rainwater filtered through stone

when I sin against it
its revenge is absence

its loss unbearable

Tipping Point

my dear one
I thought you would outlive me
I thought you would be the comfort
of my old age

I thought when I left this world
you would remain behind
your trees sheltering the earth
your canopy filled with scarlet macaws
howler monkeys   and sloths
perpetually pointing their paws
toward infinity

what will I do when you are gone
your ashes scattered
your grave unmarked?

if there is a gate that leads out
of the land of the dead
pass through it
come to me at night
wrap me in your vines
kiss me with your serpents' lips
sing me the songs of your frogs
gaze on me with lemur eyes

you are my darling
my love   my dearest friend

stay   I beg you
don't disappear

don't abandon me

Deep in the Jungle

at dawn and dusk the jungle sings

its sounds pile up
on top of one another
like the layers of a cake
the shades of its leaves
float over our faces
its frogs gather around us
its parrots flock over us
and something huge
splashes in the shallows of its rivers

could we have learned
to love one another better
if we had learned to sit quietly
until we could hear
the sound of its leaves
falling to the forest floor
blown up and down
by the breath of its trees
and the slow steady rasp
of its snakes
coiling and climbing
over prop roots and vines

what if we had valued wildness
over cities   water over fire
kissed instead of quarreling
slept in each other's arms
night after night
flesh to flesh   breath to breath
wrapped in frog song and longing

I Became Frail and Thin Like Lace

I became frail and thin like lace
rose up and rode
the circumpolar winds
saw hope rise from the ocean
in a golden column
saw orcas sinking yachts
and tigers romping with their young
saw every animal that
had ever gone extinct
gathered in a heaven of animals
their souls as beautiful
as sunsets

birds with no names
flew south
carrying me on
a carpet of feathers
beneath me lay an earth
utterly transformed
forests that had been burned
in flames of greed
rose again like columned
cathedrals

reaching down
I trailed my fingers
through their green-leafed
canopies   heard birdsong
frogsong   and the song of sap
humming through roots and twigs
like blood humming
through the veins of a great mother

reaching up

I plucked the strings of the stars
and heard them recite a poem
that spun off into space
in shining threads
like divine sugar

your life is not the only life
the stars sang
even the thing you have destroyed
will return

and the birds without names flew on
carrying me south on a carpet of feathers
toward whatever next came
next

I Will Sing Whale Songs

I will sing whale songs
I will chant with the crickets
and gather with the coyotes
to praise the moon

I will fly with the owls
turn my head around backwards
stare at the stars
with huge yellow eyes

PART V

The Winds of Cedar Street

The Winds of Cedar Street

the avocado plants droop in the sun
the pumpkins ripen in my garden
they are not moons or globes or children's mouths
or signatures or seasons
the dry grass is not a catastrophe of gold
broken by the wind
it is not your beard or hair
nor the brush of your fingers along my spine
fine and soft as so many stems

the air rises in blue columns
lifting birds and thistle down and spasms of dust
cleaning love out of the corners of things
sanding me down to the grain

A Cloak of Black Feathers

it always starts like this
my mind closing down
curling into a tight circle
that I can't escape

pain sifts over me
like a cloak of black feathers
and I feel myself sinking
into a darkness no one else can see

the paths I followed to get here
are half-erased
and the tracks that are left
lead to a pit
filled with the cries
of abandoned animals

tell me how to leave this place
tell me how to climb back
into the light

The Ephemeral River

not things
but the faded memory of things
bubbling up from the mud
softened
by great waving columns
of drowned weeds

an ephemeral river
a floating mirror
a cup you no longer
recognize as a cup
a familiar unfamiliar face

terrified by branches
startled by rain
lost in small rooms

Foster's Bighorn Cafe

moose heads
mummified bobcats
a fawn stuffed with sawdust
a walrus, a giraffe, an Indian elephant

three rooms filled with dust   fur
death and mortal terror

tell me how to escape
the memory of this memory

tell me how to resurrect the animals

tell me how to pry my head off the wall

Arabesque

Three poems for women without children

Ballerinas

the nuns sit in the Lady chapel
their faces reflect
the entire spectrum of
light streaming though
the stained glass windows
and their wimples float out
behind them like wings

all the souls of the earth
are their children
they claim

there is a motherhood they say
more expansive than
the generation of blood
there is a feeding of the
whole race
that can only be performed
in perfect silence
like the space between the water
and the fall of the water
like the absolute emptiness of a sky
broken by one perfect branch

(sometimes I think
a woman by herself
is like a breath
that can rise up and infuse
all of creation)

Pas de Deux

my mother hands me
a blue china cup
half full of milk

the ice is breaking up
on the river
she tells me
the floes catch
in her dark hair
and her hands unfold
like flowers

did you want to be a grandmother
I ask her
she gives me both her hands
in a single bouquet
and says

let me be the mother
of the mother
of the dance

Grand Jeté

some rhythms must remain unbroken

like a dancer in an
arabesque
some women cannot carry
a child
in their arms

some come to salvation
drawn by the hands of small children

some can only make their leaps

alone

PART VI

The Crazy Mongoose

Resilience, Luck, and Defiance

The Crazy Mongoose

I was Rikki-Tikki-Tavi
the crazy mongoose
the girl they could never shake

when the boys played football
in the Evan' s backyard
I tackled them and hung onto their legs
as they banged my head against the dirt
filled my mouth with crabgrass
ran with me toward the goals
like limping bears

I was 40 pounds of stubborn
40 pounds of fury
Rikki-Tikki-Tavi
the crazy little mongoose
who always brought them down

When our drunken neighbor Bill
grabbed me   lifted me into the air
and stuck his hand under my dress
I bit through his thumb
right to the bone
bitch he cried   *you little bitch!*
Rikki-Tikki-Tavi
who learned a new word
the crazy five-year-old mongoose
who got thrown into her own sandbox
and didn't mind a bit

And then there was Ethan
sixteen and a chess master

who came over to teach me
a move called “castling”
and jumped me instead
held me down on our living room rug
for a few seconds until I went mad
thrashed and snarled
slashed at him with my teeth
made hissing noises
yelled that I’d bite off any part of him
that got close to me

Rikki-Tikki-Tavi
the crazy four foot eleven
92-pound mongoose
who was willing to die
willing to go down fighting
and take a piece of his nose
with her the sharp-toothed crazy girl
who backed him off
who did not accept his apology
or soften to his tears
who wore her bruises
to high school the next day
like badges of honor

who spit every time
his name was mentioned
and never did learn to castle

The Crazy Mongoose Part II

1.
imagine Rikki
asleep in a bed in a friend's house
in a blue flannel nightgown
and fuzzy socks
awakened suddenly
by a naked stranger
crawling in beside her
a man forever nameless
from the party downstairs
slinking under the comforter
like a plucked chicken

then imagine his surprise his terror
when Rikki screams
her terrible piercing
carnivorous scream
clicking her mongoose tongue
shoving him onto the floor
and out the door
pushing him naked and wilted
into a blizzard and rattle of sleet

imagine the slamming the locking
the pounding the pleading

for God's sake give me my pants
I just wanted to have a little fun
It's five below out here!

You should have thought of that
before you jumped me! Rikki yells
And pulling out her Swiss Army knife
she flips open the scissors

and cuts his pants into one-inch strips
while the sleet rattles musically
against the window panes

2.
Or take that assistant director
working on a children's film
based on the best script Rikki ever sold
that tall skinny Hollywood guy
who lured her back to his boat
for a party that turned out not to be happening
and getting her alone   chased her around
the deck like a horny sailor

that self-proclaimed God's Gift to Women
who wouldn't take NO
for an answer until Rikki threatened
to sue him for assault
and battery and stupidity and
the ability to make women nauseous
at a distance

that guy who said
(and Rikki is not making this up)
"You'll never sell another script, baby."
And then imagine her laughing in his scrawny face
and saying "*I don't give a rat's ass.*
I have a job, a pension, and dental insurance
and if you so much as touch me
I'll take you down."

3.
Rikki's list is long, but most women's are:

The Dean of Humanities at UC Berkeley
who offered her a tenure-track position if she'd

sleep with him   and reeled back disbelieving
when she told him she'd rather
eat dry bread in a garret

The professor who
hearing Rikki tell him to back off
decided she was a "good girl"
proposed marriage, sent her roses,
followed her back to Indiana
to her mongoose lair
knelt on her parents' front steps
begged and pleaded
and declared his undying love
and became   for a few hours
a tripping hazard

Or the driver who tried to force
Rikki off the road
that laughing maniac
whose front bumper
Rikki banged into over and over again
as she remembered
the tender words of advice
her dear mother gave her
when she turned 17:
Honey, when you're in a car
you have a 3,000-pound weapon.
So use it!

Shall we count the Hells Angels
who slammed Rikki up against a wall
during The Summer of Love?
or the time Rikki bolted
through a hole in a hurricane fence
the size of a dog door
when three men cornered

her in a parking lot
and threatened
to cut her up with knives?

4.
Rikki knows she's been lucky
her stories all have
happy endings or at least
endings she can live with

she's getting old now
her teeth are blunt
and she bites her fingernails
it's been a long time
since she's played tackle football

but sometimes in her dreams
she sees a cobra coiling through the grass
powerful   deadly   rearing up to strike
and she jumps it   rides on its back
digs her teeth into its neck
screams and clicks her tongue
holds on   holds on   holds on
and brings it down

This Car Belonged to a Little Old Lady

This car belonged to a little old lady
who only drove it to church on Sundays

before she was a little old lady
she was in a covert US military operation
so black opped she couldn't see her hand
in front of her face

dropped behind enemy lines from a
Black Hawk helicopter
she gathered invaluable intelligence
that shortened a war and saved hundreds of lives
then made her way back to the front lines
shooting, stabbing, or strangling the
eight enemy soldiers who tried to kill her
and breaking with her bare hands
the neck of the man who tried to rape her

This next car also belonged to a little
old lady who only drove it to a sex club on Saturdays
before she got old she had thirty-two lovers
(although only twelve were serious affairs)

This last car belonged to
(you guessed it) a little old
lady who at the age of 80
went on a 9-state bank spree
gave the money to 27 charities
fended off a rabid grizzly
and founded a no-kill shelter
for tigers, lions, rattlesnakes, and
other exotic animals

she liked to kiss the snakes
and suck their forked tongues into her mouth
she called herself "Eve"
as in "Eve of Destruction"

(you would not have wanted to meet her in a dark alley)

PART VII

The Kama Sutra of Kindness

The Kama Sutra of Kindness

Position Number 1: Blue Silk Sheets

in ancient Japan
after the first night
poems were exchanged
between lovers

a branch of white blossoms
rests against the sky
you sleep
on my blue silk sheets

this brush brings words
to the blank rice papers
you touch me
and I speak

the third time
you enter a woman
it is mandatory
to say something kind

when I smell your hair
I think of wind and anemones

the imagination has
its own erogenous zones

your body bears me
to another season
thank you for resting
here with me
balanced on the crested moon

Position Number 2: White Birches

should I greet you
as if
we had merely eaten
together one night
when the white birches
dripped wet
and lightening etched
black trees on your walls?

it is not love
I am asking

love comes from years
of breathing
skin to skin
tangled in each other's dreams
until each night
weaves another thread
in the same web
of blood and sleep

> and I have only
> passed through you quickly
> like light
> and you have only
> surrounded me suddenly
> like flame

the lake is cold
the snows are sudden
the wild cherry bends
and winter's a burden

> in your hand I feel
> spring burn in the bud

Position Number 3: The Scent of Paperwhites

It's easy to love
through a cold spring
when the poles
of the willows
turn green
pollen falls like
a yellow curtain
and the scent of
Paper Whites
clots
the air

but to love for a lifetime
takes talent

you have to mix yourself
with the strange
beauty of someone
else
wake each morning
for 72,000
mornings in
a row so
breathed and
bound and
tangled
that you can hardly
sort out
your arms
and
legs

you have to
find forgiveness
in everything
even ink stains

and broken
cups

you have to be willing to move through
life
together
the way the long
grasses move
in a field
when you careen
blindly toward
the other
side

there's never going to be anything
straight or predictable
about your path
except the
flattening
and the springing
back

you just go on walking for years
hand in hand
waist deep in the weeds
bent slightly forward
like two question
marks
and all the while it
burns
my dear
it burns beautifully above
you
and goes on
burning
like a relentless
sun

Position Number 4: A Delta of Fingers

near the end of a long day
when time stretches out in a delta of fingers
that grasps at currents and sand
we will lie side by side
listening to the cawing of crows
and the sound of sap
pulsing through the trees
wicking the willow wands back to life

after the endless eclipse of living
we will feel light course through our bodies again
as we trace the geography of our flesh
with our fingertips
outlining the continents of our shoulders
the hills of our hips the rivers of our spines

outside   bare twigs
will click against half-budded branches
and a warm wind will rise and fall
as we lie together   sheltering each other
from the griefs that have scarred us
and the sadnesses
that have seemed perpetual

as the last pale sun of spring
pours in through the blinds
gilding our faces
with long golden bands
I will breathe in your breath
and you will breathe in mine

Position Number 5: Two Blue-winged Macaws

a river of molten glass
paved with fine white sand
and on the far bank
a thousand trees
eternally burning
eternally throwing themselves
into the sky

look
we are two blue-winged macaws
frozen in mid-flight over a wall of green fire
strangers lost in the jungle of each other's bodies

lovers who don't want to be found

Night Comb

when I smell your hair
I dream of almond blossoms
the slow drift of cedar smoke
pale golden trees sitting
in dark pools   sleeping birds
and heavy slick leaves
large as my tongue

your hair lingers in my hands
like the touch of a silk blanket
tingles between my fingers
like a fine spray
I want to dive into it
follow in its wake
until I am lost and tangled in it
the way a great forest
is lost and tangled in its trees
the way an ocean is lost and
tangled in itself
the way we are lost and tangled
in each other each night
in kindness   bliss   and sleep

Walking Toward the Largo do Machado

when the smell of jasmine
flows through the streets of Catete like a warm fog
when the scent is so liquid you can
breathe it in   get drunk and stagger
I think of all the years I have loved you
and all the years I will go on loving you
I think of how we protect each other from pain and betrayal
how each night we wrap ourselves around each other
and peace floats above our bed like a canopy of white petals

I Have Gathered Your Body

I have gathered your body
from the forest floor

like bloodroot you rise
above the leaf-mesh of winter

tongues of fire
explode from your breast
spreading in slow motion
crowning the pines
with incandescent light

No Past Tenses

your breath is a warm mist
that envelops us
like a transparent balloon
rising toward a sky so blue
it bands the horizon with purple

you bend over   pick up a handful of sand
sift it between your palms
watch it fall in a silent pile
between our bare feet

you brush my forehead with your lips
I smooth down your eyebrows with my thumbs
run my fingers through the silk of your hair
we hold hands   take deep breaths

the current glitters and curls
the willow leaves blow silver
the dust on the far bank
pulses and trembles
the river flows west toward the sea

today
in this place that does not exist
on this afternoon that does not number hours
we know neither fear nor regret
nor what has happened
nor what will happen

golden light surrounds us
we laugh for no reason at all

White Gauze Curtains

in them we see
the dead we have loved
blowing toward us
with outstretched hands

how unsubstantial they are
how beautiful in their flight
as they advance and retreat
struggling for purchase

In This Burning World

on the long road down the hill
the cobblestones tip us like drunken sailors
under a sky smeared with volcanic dust

at the bottom lies a sea
clear and pale as the skin
beneath our arms

in this burning world
where we can never stop to rest
you reach out and brush
the tips of my fingers

our parched skin flakes off
in tiny bits and floats up toward the sun
riding the great cone-shaped thermals
of this slowly turning planet

we are two birds
gliding through an empty sky
lost   uncertain
filled with unreasonable joy

PART VIII

Tiger of Fire/Tiger of Flame

Tiger of Fire/Tiger of Flame

tiger of fire   tiger of flame
you who prowl the jungles
you who prowl the deserts
you who walk across oceans as if they were paths
you whose claws melt the ice of high mountains
you whose eyes burn sunsets
you whose tongue is the forge of stars

tiger of fire   tiger of flame
creator of light   creator of Earth
you who walk silently among us
you whose spine is molten
you whose breath is the sun
you who are the end of our beginning
you who are the beginning of our end
you who know all bushes are burning bushes

tiger of fire   tiger of flame
we walk as you every time we walk
we dream as you every time we dream
every time we speak   we speak as you
every time we think   we are nothing but you
burning with life   burning with desire

tiger of fire   tiger of flame
deep in the jungle of our brains
deep in the jungle of our hearts
your fire rises up our backbones
your fire smolders under our feet
your fire runs down our legs
caresses our fingertips
plays over our lips

tiger of fire   tiger of flame
you who blind us with longing
you who blind us with love
you who burn in us forever
with the light of creation

NOTES

"The Long Warm Tongue of Your Future" Jaguars have thirty teeth. Humans have thirty-two.

"Here/Not Here" The origin of this poem is strange. I wrote it on January 30, 2020, about, a month before I first heard of COVID-19, and about six weeks before the first US shutdown on March 15th. I have no logical explanation for this.

"Back In 2020" This poem was written on May 1, 2020, after eight weeks of sheltering in place from COVID-19.

"Tipping Point" According to Luciana Gatti at Brazil's National Institute for Space Research,satellite photos indicate that, due to deforestation, we may be five years from a pointof no return when 40% of the Amazonian rainforest will irreversibly begin to convert into dry savannah.

"The Ephemeral River," Ephemeral rivers only have flowing water for a short duration during and after rainfall. They are above the water table, not fed by ground water, and are often found in arid or semi-arid regions.

"The Crazy Mongoose." In a game of chess, "castling" is a special move that allows a player to move two pieces at once. The move is named after the rook, a chess piece that looks like a castle.

"The Kama Sutra of Kindness: Position Number 2: White Birches," The author is grateful to Poet Hillary Frasier Hayes who has called this poem "one of the most magnificent poems ever written in English."

The following poems were first published in Mary Mackey's previous collections:

"The Kama Sutra of Kindness: Position Number 1: Blue Silk Sheets" and "The Kama Sutra of Kindness: Position Number 2: White Birches" in *Skin Deep* (Arlington VA: Gallimaufry Press, 1978).

"Arabesque," "Night Comb," and "Cytheria" in *The Dear Dance of Eros* (Seattle WA: Fjord Press, 1987).

"The Kama Sutra of Kindness: Position Number 3: The Scent of Paperwhites" in *Breaking The Fever* (New York, NY: Marsh Hawk Press, 2006).

"Walking Toward the Largo do Machado" in *Travelers With No Ticket Home* (New York, NY: Marsh Hawk Press, 2014)

"In This Burning World," in *The Jaguars That Prowl Our Dreams: New and Selected Poems 1974 to 2018* (New York, NY: Marsh Hawk Press, 2018)

ACKNOWLEDGMENTS

Thanks to Thomas Fink whose insightful editorial suggestions were invaluable and to Sandy McIntosh and designer Susan Quasha who worked tirelessly to prepare *In This Burning World* for publication. I am also grateful to Pamela Berkman and Dorothy Hearst who gave me companionship, support, and critical feedback; Mike Baltar, Josiah Patterson, Lee Watson, Ruth Watson, and Oswaldo Vargas—all members of Books Beer & Bread; and to the members of the WELL; The Women's National Book Association, San Francisco Chapter; Joyce Jenkins, editor of *Poetry Flash*; Richard Loranger; Godfrey McIntire; Mara Keller; Raymond Smith and Patricia Gama Ramsden; Lise Sedrez, Sandro Dutra e Silva, and Janice Haag. Special thanks also to Allan Hoben who welcomed me to his home in Maine and gave me time, silence, inspiration, and encouragement in the middle of the boreal forests of Cape Split as I finished revising the poems in this collection, and to his daughter Alice Hoben, who became my friend and walking companion. Finally, I would like to thank my late husband Angus Wright for his unfailing affection, encouragement, inspiration, and support for nearly forty years. Many of the poems in this collection were inspired by the time he and I spent in Mexico and Brazil.

I also wish to express my gratitude to the editors of the periodicals and anthologies in which some of the poems in this collection first appeared:

"The Temple of Bel," *Escape Wheel,* great weather for MEDIA anthology 2020. ed. Jane Ormerod *et al.* (New York, NY 2020), Pg. 142.

"Hurricane/Huracán," *The Marsh Hawk Press Review* (Spring 2021), ed. Eileen Tabios https://marshhawkpress.org/the-marsh-hawk-press-review/

"Here/Not Here," *arriving at a shoreline,* great weather for MEDIA anthology 2022, ed. Jane Ormerod *et al.* (New York, NY 2022). Pg. 40.

"The Kama Sutra of Kindness: Position Number 3: The Scent of Paperwhites" and "Walking Toward The Lago do Machado" *Marsh Hawk Press Review* (Spring 2023), ed. Thomas Fink https://marshhawkpress.org/the-marsh-hawk-press-review/

“The Crazy Mongoose,” *Mosaic: The Sitting Room Anthology,* Spring 2023, ed. Sharon Bard, Karen Peterson, J.J. Wilson (The Sitting Room Press; Penngrove CA, 2023). p. 31.

“Mocking Cassandra,” *The Tule Review*, Summer 2023, ed. Susan Kelly DeWitt (Sacramento Poetry Center Press; Sacramento CA, 2023). Pg. 59.

“Pillar of Smoke/Pillar of Fire,” *Persimmon Tree,* Summer 2024, ed. Andrea Carter Brown
https://persimmontree.org/summer-2024/poetry-of-western-states/

“The Prophecy of The Trees,” *The Tule Review*, Fall 2024. ed. Linda Jackon Collins, (Sacramento Poetry Center Press; Sacramento CA, 2024).

“White Gauze Curtains,” *Plume Magazine*, Issue #159, November 2024, ed. Daniel Lawless. https://plumepoetry.com/white-gauze-curtains/

“The Crystal Falcon,” and “The Emperor Contemplates His Solitude,” *Resistance: A Journal of Radical Environmental Humanities*, Fall 2025, ed. Marco Amiero (University of Nebraska Press: Lincoln NE) https://nebraskapressjournals.unl.edu/journal/resistance-a-journal-of-radical-environmental-humanities/

“The Winds of Cedar Street,” *The Berkeley Anthology*, ed. Joyce Jenkins (Manic D Press; Berkeley CA, 2025).

ABOUT THE AUTHOR

Mary Mackey became a writer by running high fevers, tramping through tropical jungles, being swarmed by army ants, and reading. She is the author of eight previous poetry collections, including *Sugar Zone,* winner of a PEN Award, and *The Jaguars That Prowl Our Dreams*, winner of a Women's Spirituality Book Award from the California Institute of Integral Studies and the 2019 Eric Hoffer Award for Best Book Published by a Small Press. Wendell Berry, Jane Hirshfield, D. Nurkse, Al Young, Rafael Jesús González, Daniel Lawless, and Maxine Hong Kingston have praised her poetry for its beauty, precision, originality, and extraordinary range.

She is also the author of three co-written, prize-winning screenplays and fourteen novels, including The New York Times bestseller *A Grand Passion.* Her first novel, *Immersion* (Shameless Hussy Press, 1972), was apparently the first novel in the world published by a Second Wave Feminist Press.

Mackey's works have been translated into thirteen foreign languages including Japanese, Hebrew, Russian, Greek, Finnish, and Arabic. She is past president of the West Coast branch of PEN; a Fellow of the Virginia Center for the Creative Arts; and a member of the National Book Critics Circle, The Women's National Book Association, The Writers Guild of America, West, and SOLCHA (Sociedad Latinoamericana y Caribeña de Historia Ambiental/Latin American and Caribbean Society of Environmental History).

A Professor Emerita of English at California State University, Sacramento, she was one of the founders of the CSUS Creative Writing Program and the CSUS Women's Studies Program. For over 25 years she traveled to Brazil with her late husband, Angus Wright, who wrote about land reform and environmental issues.

To contact her, sample more of her work, read her blog interview series *People Who Make Books Happen*, and receive her quarterly newsletter, please visit her website at https://www.marymackey.com.

On X (formerly known as Twitter) she is at @MMackeyAuthor; on Bluesky at @marymackeyauthor.bsky.social, and on Facebook at https://www.facebook.com/marymackeywriter. Her books are available in hard copy as well as in e-book and Audible editions.

Mary Mackey's literary papers are archived in the Sophia Smith Special Collections Library, Smith College, Northampton, MA. https://findingaids.smith.edu/repositories/2/resources/1222

Her collection of rare editions of small press poetry books is archived in the Smith College Mortimer Rare Book Collection.

Titles From Marsh Hawk Press

Jane Augustine *Arbor Vitae; Krazy; Night Lights; A Woman's Guide to Mountain Climbing*
Tom Beckett *~~Dipstick~~ (Diptych)*
William Benton *Light on Water*
Sigman Byrd *Under the Wanderer's Star*
Patricia Carlin: *Original Green; Quantum Jitters; Second Nature*
Claudia Carlson *The Elephant House; My Chocolate Sarcophagus; Pocket Park*
Lorna Dee Cervantes: *April on Olymbia*
Meredith Cole *Miniatures*
Jon Curley *The Installation of Fear; Hybrid Moments; Scorch Marks; Remnant Halo*
Joanne D. Dwyer *RASA*
Neil de la Flor *Almost Dorothy; An Elephant's Memory of Blizzards*
Chard deNiord *Sharp Golden Thorn*
Sharon Dolin *Serious Pink*
Joanne Dominique Dwyer *Rasa*
Steve Fellner *Blind Date with Cavafy; The Weary World Rejoices*
Thomas Fink *Zeugma, Selected Poems & Poetic Series; Joyride; Peace Conference; Clarity and Other Poems; After Taxes; Gossip*
Thomas Fink and Maya D. Mason *A Pageant for Every Addiction*
Norman Finkelstein *Inside the Ghost Factory; Passing Over*
Edward Foster *A Looking-Glass for Traytors; The Beginning of Sorrows; Dire Straits; Mahrem: Things Men Should Do for Men; Sewing the Wind; What He Ought to Know*
Paolo Javier *The Feeling is Actual*
Burt Kimmelman *Abandoned Angel; Somehow; Steeple at Sunrise; Zero Point Poiesis;* with Fred Caruso *The Pond at Cape May Point*
Basil King *Disparate Beasts: Part Two; 77 Beasts; Disparate Beasts; Mirage; The Spoken Word / The Painted Hand from Learning to Draw / A History*
Martha King *Imperfect Fit*
David Lehman *The Birth of* The Best
Phillip Lopate *At the End of the Day*
Mary Mackey *Breaking the Fever; The Jaguars That Prowl Our Dreams; Sugar Zone; Travelers With No Ticket Home; Creativity*
Jason McCall *Dear Hero*
Sandy McIntosh *The After-Death History of My Mother; Between Earth and Sky; Cemetery Chess; Ernesta, in the Style of the Flamenco; Forty-Nine Guaranteed Ways to Escape Death; A Hole In the Ocean; Lesser Lights; Obsessional; Plan B:*
Stephen Paul Miller *Any Lie You Tell Will Be the Truth; The Bee Flies in May; Fort Dad; Skinny Eighth Avenue; There's Only One God and You're Not It*
Daniel Morris *Blue Poles; Bryce Passage; Hit Play; If Not for the Courage*
Gail Newman *Blood Memory*
Geoffrey O'Brien *Where Did Poetry Come From; The Blue Hill*
Sharon Olinka *The Good City*
Christina Olivares *No Map of the Earth Includes Stars*
Justin Petropoulos *Eminent Domain*
Paul Pines *Charlotte Songs; Divine Madness; Gathering Sparks; Last Call at the Tin Palace*
Jacquelyn Pope *Watermark*
George Quasha *Things Done for Themselves*
Karin Randolph *Either She Was*
Rochelle Ratner *Balancing Acts; Ben Casey Days; House and Home*
Michael Rerick *In Ways Impossible to Fold*
Corrine Robins *Facing It; One Thousand Years; Today's Menu*
Liane Strauss *The Flaws in the Story*
Eileen R. Tabios *The Inventor: A Poet's Transcolonial Autobiography; Because I Love You I Become War; The Connoisseur of Alleys; I Take Thee, English, for My Beloved; The In(ter)vention of the Hay(na)ku; The Light Sang as It Left Your Eyes; Reproductions of the Empty Flagpole; Sun Stigmata; The Thorn Rosary* with j/j hastain *The Relational Elations of Orphaned Algebra*
Tony Trigilio: *Proof Something Happened; Craft: A Memoir*
Susan Terris *Green Leaves Unseeing; Familiar Tense; Ghost of Yesterday; Natural Defenses*
Lynne Thompson *Fretwork*
Madeline Tiger *Birds of Sorrow and Joy*
Tana Jean Welch *Latest Volcano*
Harriet Zinnes: D*rawing on the Wall; Light Light or the Curvature of the Earth; New and Selected Poems; Weather is Whether; Whither Nonstopping*
Xiaoqiu Qiu: *Other Side of Ocean* (anthology) *On Becoming a Poet*

YEAR	AUTHOR	TITLE	JUDGE
2004	Jacquelyn Pope	*Watermark*	Marie Ponsot
2005	Sigman Byrd	*Under the Wanderer's Star*	Gerald Stern
2006	Steve Fellner	*Blind Date with Cavafy*	Denise Duhamel
2007	Karin Randolph	*Either She Was*	David Shapiro
2008	Michael Rerick	*In Ways Impossible to Fold*	Thylias Moss
2009	Neil de la Flor	*Almost Dorothy*	Forrest Gander
2010	Justin Petropoulos	*Eminent Domain*	Anne Waldman
2011	Meredith Cole	*Miniatures*	Alicia Ostriker
2012	Jason McCall	*Dear Hero,*	Cornelius Eady
2013	Tom Beckett	*~~Dipstick~~ (Diptych)*	Charles Bernstein
2014	Christina Olivares	*No Map of the Earth Includes Stars*	Brenda Hillman
2015	Tana Jean Welch	*Latest Volcano*	Stephanie Strickland
2016	Robert Gibb	*After*	Mark Doty
2017	Geoffrey O'Brien	*The Blue Hill*	Meena Alexander
2018	Lynne Thompson	*Fretwork*	Jane Hirshfield
2019	Gail Newman	*Blood Memory*	Marge Piercy
2020	Tony Trigilio	*Proof Something Happened*	Susan Howe
2021	Joanne D. Dwyer	*Rasa*	David Lehman
2022	Brian Cochran	*Translation Zone*	John Yau
2023	Liane Strauss	*The Flaws in the Story*	Mary Jo Bang
2024	Xiaoqiu Qiu	*Other Side of Ocean*	John Keene